When I Was a Kid

(A sleep inductive read for Seniors)

Tommy Oldfarte

For Pearl and Alick (alias mum and dad) …

and to my son, Blake

Contents

The Backyard

When I was a kid and mum and dad was doin' it hard
We always had the joy of our own backyard.
It was hallowed ground where footies soared,
wickets tumbled.
 Where speckies were grabbed and slips catches fumbled.

There was a basketball ring, a wash-house and loo
Some lawn and a garden where mum's veggies grew.
A Hill's hoist took over from the old washing line
And a tumble-down shed was in happy decline.

There was Howie and Robert and Dennis and me
And we owned that shed from late arvo 'till tea.
It was dusty and dim and a haven to spiders …
But we made it our fort, off-limits to outsiders.

When all else failed we were easily inspired
By dad's rusting old truck, unlicensed and flat-tired.
The door-hinges creaked as we scrambled inside
And hit the road for a *fantastical* ride!

Sometimes we'd play allies for keeps or for fun
And Tinka, our dog, he just loved to run.
We'd laugh, we'd wrestle, we'd clamber and fall
And climb over palings to retrieve a lost ball.

Surrounded by fences, the house and the lane
I dream of our backyard again and again.
So to me mum and dad, on behalf of us kids …
Thanks for the memories, I wouldn't swap 'em for quids.

The Day the Dunny Burned

When I was a kid, and I'm not bein' funny -
Every home had an outdoor dunny.
Ours had a trellis in peelin' white paint
With a bit of a lean it was kinda quaint.
There were five of us kids, money was sparse
We used last week's News to wipe our … backsides!

My eldest brother was a bit of a wag -
And he'd sneak to the dunny to have a drag.
With a smoke and a comic he'd sit alone
Forgettin' all else while he hogged the throne.
On one such occasion dad's patience wore thin
And he yelled to my brother … *ya better come in*!

Daryl up and stubbed the smouldering smoke
T'ween the boards of the dunny, that was no joke -
'Cos when dad ventured out with the racing paper
He smelt wood burning and cried … *what's this caper*!
With his daks half down, he up and took flight …
The dunny's on fire, the boy set it alight!

The fire brigade came with their sirens blarin'
Dad just stood there, cursin' and swearin'
My brother had scampered, he was *in the poo*
Till mum said to Dad … Alick, *let's get an indoor loo*!
So all was forgiven, my brother returned
And that's how it was … *the day the dunny burned*!

The Multi-coloured Poof

When I was a kid, we had a poof
Now please, just let me say …
When I was a kid a poof didn't mean
You know.
A poof was made from vinyl
It was usually round and squat
Our poof was multi-coloured
And stuffed with goodness knows what.

It was in shades of black and yellow
As far as I recall
And was moved about the lounge room –
Used by one and all.
Poofs were an essential item
In houses around our way
But Mrs. Hob-Knob, up the street –
She called her poof … a poo-fay!

My brother sat upon the poof
With his tea juggled on his lap
Watching Disneyland on Sunday night
While dad just had a nap.

But Monday's it was different
T.V. Ringside came on late
With a ciggy, a beer and the poof at his feet
Dad thought that show was great.

Our poof's glory days were numbered
And it came as no surprise
That my sister's little buggers
Were the cause of its demise.
While playing superheroes
And bringing to life their dreams
They used the poof as a landing base
And burst it at the seams!

Pigeons 12 O'clock High

When I was easily led
My brother persuasively said:
"Those pigeons you know,
They've just got to go …
'Cos things have come to a head."

The trouble was nothing new
It was all about pigeon poo.
Mum's lovely, clean washing
Was taking a sploshing …
There was only one thing to do.

The slug gun was cleaned and dusted
My brother was keen as mustard
As we looked to the sky
He yelled, "twelve o'clock high!"
And that's when we two were busted.

Our neighbour, he stormed through the gate
By jingo he was very irate
So my brother and me
We decided to flee –
Leaving mum to look after our fate.

She leant the old bloke her ear
Then she said, "Now listen my dear.
Your pigeons are pooing
And my tempers fair stewing
So you better clear off outta here!"

Bluey Busts Out

When I was just a little kid,
And this is ridgey-didge –
We had a budgie called Bluey,
And he lived on the kitchen fridge.

He strutted in his wire cage
Complete with mirror and swing
From there he would prune his feathers
And squawk, and talk and sing.

Bluey had a vocabulary,
It was limited I have to say.
He could coin a phrase, chirp his name
And even tweet, g'day!

Sometimes we'd let our Bluey
Fly around the house
He'd sit on your finger, nibble your ear
And eat cheddar like a mouse.

Dad came home one evening
After a beer or three or four
"I'm here," he said. "The bird!" We cried

As Bluey flew out the door.

We thought he'd gone forever
But mum said, "Just a minute.
I'll put an ad in the paper …
Now what should we say in it?"

You can imagine our excitement
Disbelief and all
When a car pulled up,
A lady jumped out
And Bluey let out his call …

"Mum, I'm home!"

She's Right, It's Cracker Night

When I was a kid … fireworks weren't put on for show –
Fireworks meant **cracker night** and kids would spend
their dough
On thr'penny bangers and Tom Thumbs and sparklers
and spinning wheels
And mums and dads would come along for the laughter,
the cheers and squeals!

We built our bonny on the vacant block behind the library
and tennis courts
Any danger of houses catching fire was, well, furthest
from our thoughts.
Household rubbish, old tyres, boxes, dried out garden
cuttings and more -
It all went on the bonfire, including one year …
someone's dunny door!

Guy Fawkes was the star of course and he sat atop the
towering pyre -
Dressed in pyjamas stashed with newspaper – just waiting
to be set on fire.

A dash of kero, a lighted match and whoosh and
> up he went ...
And then the crackers would pop and bang and
> skyrockets would be heaven sent.

There were wars between us kids of course with crackers
> tossed like dynamite
We were lucky no-one was hurt, although one year our
> dog took off in fright.
Like some ancient tribe we laughed and danced in the
> fiery glow
Until a parent brought out the hose and said ...
> *Sorry kids, it's time to go.*

A Dog of a Concert

When I was a kid, a career in show biz beckoned
A star would be born, or so my grandma reckoned.
The Sunday school concert was to be my launching pad
And people would say … I used to know him as a lad.

The plan was flawed I knew that from the start
I feared forgetting my lines, or worse, letting go a fart!
My role was humble, my face hidden by a mask
To mimic a little doggy was my designated task.

Mum laboured for hours to produce my canine cossie
A hat adorned my head – in a somewhat precarious posie
A cellophane window covered the open front
Inside was a picture of a dog – a wiry, little runt.

A familiar song would cue my entry onto the stage
How Much Is That Doggy in the Window – it was all the
rage
Woof, woof were the two little words I had to utter
Gran said: Bark them out loud boy, don't mumble or
stutter.

The curtain rose, the audience cheered and now I had my
                                                    chance
But my throat dried up, I lost my nerve, and quickly wet
                                                  my pants!
I never trod the boards again, some things aren't meant
                                                    to be
The trouble is, since acting the dog … I lift my leg to pee!

A Shot in the Arm

When I was a kid, polio was a crippling disease
But the Salk vaccine helped put parent's minds at ease
Kids of course were not so quick to understand
The benefits of that dreaded jab from the doctor's hand.

And so it was we lined the corridor at the bottom of
the stairs
And stood like sacrificial lambs in trembling pairs
A makeshift curtain was visible at the far end of the hall
As shadowy figures secretly prepared for one and all.

Heather was the first to enter this nightmarish dream
Would it hurt we wondered, then we heard her
banshee-like scream
John was sick and Peter tried to run
Allan almost fainted, this would not be fun.

Pale-faced and teary-eyed
Heather re-emerged with a glint of pride
Triumphant she walked passed our curious faces
And one by one we took a few nervous paces.

I saw a man hold something shiny up to the light
A woman in a crisp white dress did nothing to relieve
                                              my plight
Hello son, said the man, seeming aware of my stress
Roll up your sleeve said the crisp white dress.

She rubbed my arm with disinfected cotton wool
This won't hurt said the man – ouch! - what a load of bull!
I looked away as the needle pierced my skin
Have a lolly smiled the nurse – and she handed me the tin.

French With a Twist

When I was a kid, French and Latin were taught at school
And dad said … *whoever thought of that is a dead-set fool –*
They should teach you Italian, he complained bitterly.
Cripes, he said, *there's more I-tyes here than in Italy*!

You won't be learnin' Latin, dad said in haste …
Unless you join the clergy it's a flippin *waste!*
So French won out and I fronted up in my long socks
and short pants
And our teacher, Miss Layer, she pointed to the map
and said *–this is France.*

Miss Layer was a woman of considerable size
To be a distraction in her class was …
well, extremely unwise.
She cruised the aisle like a battleship on the high sea
Quiet but deadly she would aim a well-used
textbook at me!

Thwack! And the back of my head would ring like the
bells of St. Mary's
Sorry lad, she would say,
but it seems you've been away with the fairies!
Needless to mention, French failed me, or maybe
I failed it.
Whatever the case, Miss Layer more than did her bit.

In later years, when I was still unworldly and young
I visited France and spoke in the native tongue
The butcher tried to understand me of course …
But the rump chops he sold me, they weren't cow …
they was horse!

A Billyful of Milk

When I was a kid, there was a comforting sound
The gentle, **clipperty-clop** as the milko did his round
Warm in bed I would hear the horse and cart
Rolling down the street with the occasional stop and start

At the milkman's command, either a whistle or a whoa!
The trusty old horse would stop or go
And the milk was poured, all frothy and white
Into dew-dripping billies left out overnight.

The Milkman would run from house to house
Quick as a cat and quiet as a mouse!
If money was tight, mum would leave him a note –
Just half a billy please, is what she would have wrote.

Once in a while I would be early to rise
And I'd wait on the veranda, rubbing my eyes
The Milko would smile and say, *g'day son*
And I'd carry the milk down the passage to mum.

It would slop in waves from side to side
And mum would joke that she'd tan my hide —
Don't spill a drop … she'd threaten in jest
As I carefully clutched that old billy to my chest.

Then she'd warm some milk for me to sip
And laugh at the **mo** on my upper lip
We would sit in the kitchen, just us two …
'Till mum would say … *now, it's school for you*!

Have You Got Your Hanky?

When I was a kid, I used to get cranky
When mum would holler ... *have you got your hanky?*
My friends would snigger and they'd mimic my mum
I was the butt of their jokes, it wasn't much fun.

Mum was a wealth of those helpful homilies
Some were true ... others were anomalies!
She would whip 'em out at the drop of a hat
But "mum" was the word, you daren't argue with that.

Are you wearing clean undies ... dear mum would fuss
Heaven forbid if you're knocked down by a bus.
Now as if the doctor would be so shirty ...
I can't treat him ... his damn undies are dirty!

Your shoes are a disgrace, mum would admonish
You hurry inside and give them a polish.
Have you brushed your teeth? Let's see your nails ...
Mum was a stickler for the finer details.

She combed my hair and *Bryl-Creamed* it down
And flicked my ear at the first hint of a frown
She straightened my socks and tucked in my shirt …
Threatened to kill me if I played in the dirt.

I had to go out looking so *Spic and Span*!
Anything less and you know what hit the fan.
I loved my mum and would never deflate her
I was the cleanest kid south of the equator!

All's Fair in Love and Cricket

When I was a kid, I loved my sport
The trouble was I was kinda short
Be patient said mum, one day you'll grow
Just give it your best and have a go.

I tried my hand at playing cricket -
Found myself on a sticky wicket
The pads were as big as I was small
The bowler stood about ten feet tall.

I closed my eyes, I swung and I missed
That's my slow ball, he laughingly hissed
He thundered in and I snicked a four
He raised his eyebrows and dropped his jaw.

Like a raging bull he marked his run
He turned and charged, I thought I was done
I felt my skin go cold and clammy
But bugger me, he did his hammy.

He managed to get the ball away –
A head-high full-toss I have to say
I ducked in time and thank God it missed …
But it hit the keeper where he'd never been kissed.

Pandemonium filled the air
The opposition they cried … *unfair!*
We stole a single and pinched the game
That was my moment of cricketing fame.

About the Author

Rod McLure (*Tommy Oldfarte*) was 16 when a bloke on a bicycle arrived with a telegram telling him to go along to the local radio station - 3GL, Geelong - for a job interview. It hadn't occurred to Rod to pursue a career in or on the wireless. It just happened. He never got to sit behind a microphone. Instead, he found himself behind a typewriter, writing commercials … for twenty years!

There was a two-year break living in London and Kombieing around Europe. Then followed two marriages, three Scottish terriers, becoming a dad at age 57and working in aged care and disability.

Rod has written a few one-act plays and covered the football, writing as an old lady called, "Dotty".

Rod says that he is trying his hardest to grow up. (*A work in progress, we wish him well*). However, we have a feeling it could be a case of … once a kid, always a kid.

Acknowledgments

Rod would like to acknowledge and give thanks to the "voices" that have helped him with his writing over the years.

There was young "Titch" whose diary of going to the footy with his gran back in 1963 was a feature in the local paper throughout the 2005 football season.

This was followed by an old dear named "Dotty" who covered the football for two seasons in a column called "Dotty On the Cats!"

And of course, that old bugger, Bert, who whinged to everyone over the air on *Ace Radio* in Victoria's Western District.

Now "Tommy Oldfarte" has joined the club.

Rod would like to thank them all because without their help, well … he would be lost for words.

P.S. A special thank you to Ian Hooper and the crew at Book Reality.